I Love
Owls

By Steve Parker
Illustrated by Andrea Morandi

Miles Kelly

First published in 2007 by Miles Kelly Publishing Ltd
Bardfield Centre, Great Bardfield, Essex, CM7 4SL, UK

This edition printed in 2009

4 6 8 10 9 7 5 3

Editorial Director Belinda Gallagher
Art Director Jo Brewer
Assistant Editor Lucy Dowling
Creative Artworker Rick Caylor
Cover Artworker Stephan Davis
Production Manager Elizabeth Brunwin
Reprographics Stephan Davis, Liberty Newton

ISBN 978-1-84236-823-7

Printed in China

British Library Cataloguing-in-Publication Data
A catalogue record for this book is available
from the British Library

www.mileskelly.net   info@mileskelly.net

www.factsforprojects.com
The one-stop homework helper —
pictures, facts, videos, projects and more

Contents

Tawny owl

Tawny is a colour – a sort of orange-reddish brown. Many owls are tawny, but only one is called the tawny owl. In the breeding season, the male calls out as he returns with food for the female and chicks.

Too fluffy to fly

Owl chicks have soft, fluffy feathers to keep them warm. They grow stronger feathers when they are ready to fly.

Tawny owls prefer to live in the countryside but they can also be found living in tree holes around towns and villages.

These owls sometimes make their homes in magpie and squirrel nests.

The chicks stay in their nest for about three months and then fly away.

Little owl

Little owls can be found all over the world. They like to make their homes in tall towers and quiet surroundings. By day they rest and at night they hunt in parks, gardens and fields.

Worms, beetles and slugs are the favourite food of little owls.

Little owls come out to hunt just before it gets dark. This makes it easier for people to spot them.

Small and short

The well-named little owl is quite a bit smaller than a pigeon, or even a blackbird.

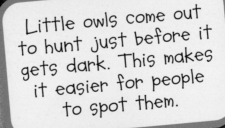

Most little owls are brown in colour with white specks. They have feathery feet and legs and yellow eyes.

This owl has a loud call that can travel a long way in the night air.

Snowy owl

Most owls fly at night. However, the snowy owl flies in daylight, too. This is because it lives in the Arctic. During the short Arctic summer the Sun never sets and there is no darkness at all!

As there are no trees in the Arctic, the snowy owl has to make its home on the ground.

While the male owl goes hunting, the female stays behind and looks after the chicks.

The male hunts for mice, voles, rats, rabbits, and many kinds of small birds.

Whoo's whoo?

Most female and male owls look similar. The male snowy owl has fewer dark specks than the female — he is almost pure white.

Barn owl

Barn owls do not just nest in barns.
They also rest and nest in church
towers, old buildings, hollow
trees and caves in cliffs.
They can be found in
many different parts
of the world, from
cold mountains to
tropical forests.

Too bright
Barn owls swoop on
animals injured by cars on
roads. They may get blinded
by the headlights and not
be able to fly away.

Long, sharp claws
called talons help the
barn owl to catch its
food each night.

The snow-white
feathers make the
owl look like a ghost
in the moonlight.

The barn owl swoops
silently through the air.
Its prey cannot hear it
until it is too late.

Voles and mice
make a tasty
midnight snack
for the barn owl.

Scops owl

The scops owl makes a loud 'chiup' sound. The sound can go on and on, and may even keep people awake at night. This is why it is also known as the screech owl. Even though it makes so much noise, the scops owl is very difficult to see as its feathers blend in with its surroundings.

When a scops owl is out in the open, it stays perfectly still, so it can't be seen.

Owl pellets

An owl cannot eat the hard bones, claws and beaks in its food. So it coughs these bits up, all pressed together into a lump called a pellet.

Great horned owl

The great horned owl has tufts of feathers on its head. They look like horns, or ears. However an owl's actual ears are hidden by its feathers. An owl can hear as well as it can see.

The male great horned owl makes a deep hooting noise. This warns other owls to stay away.

Big eyes!
Make an owl mask from card. Ask an adult to help you cut out areas for the eyes. See how big they are – bigger than yours!

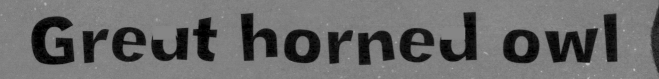

Owls cannot move their eyes from side to side. They have to move their whole head.

When it has caught its food, the owl uses its powerful hooked beak to tear up mice, rats and rabbits.

Eagle owl

The eagle owl is so big and strong that it hunts other hunters. It may catch another owl, like a tawny, or a bigger hunting bird such as a buzzard or goshawk, that is sleeping on a branch.

Ear tufts help hide the owl in its surroundings.

The owl's long, sharp claws stab into its victim like curved nails.

The eagle owl is the biggest member of the owl family. It needs lots of open space to hunt for food.

Eagle owls can hunt large animals and have been known to attack small deer and even foxes.

Big owl
The eagle owl is such a fierce hunter that even real eagles keep out of its way.

Fishing owl

Many owls hunt over land. Fishing owls prefer to fly over rivers and lakes in the moonlight. They look and listen for ripples and bubbles, which are signs of fish or similar creatures just beneath the water's surface. In order to catch their prey, fishing owls do not mind getting their feet wet!

Fishing owls stretch out their legs when flying over water. This helps them catch fish and frogs.

Wading in water

Owls do not always swoop from the air. The fishing owl may go paddling in shallow water, using its feet to help it find food.

These owls sometimes grab young rabbits that come to the water's edge for a drink.

The owl's toes are covered in tiny scales that help it to grip smooth, wriggly fish.

The fishing owl's legs have no feathers on them. This stops the owl from getting too wet and heavy.

19

Elf owl

The elf owl is one of the smallest owls.
It would fit in the palm of your hand. Even
though it is small, the owl has little to fear
when at home. It nests in a prickly cactus.

The elf owl has a short tail and very tiny feet. Unlike most other owls it does not have ear tufts.

Both female and male elf owls sit on their eggs to keep them warm.

Fierce food!

An owl's meals often fight back when caught! Worms wriggle, beetles and crickets kick and spiders bite.

The female elf owl lays up to three tiny eggs, hardly bigger than grapes.

The elf owl is too small to hunt mice. Its main meals are moths, grubs, caterpillars, crickets and beetles.

21

Boobook owl

The boobook owl is named after the 'booo-book' sound it makes. It is often found in villages and towns and usually hunts at night. However when the boobook owl has chicks, it sometimes needs to hunt during the day, too.

The male and female owls call softly to each other as they get ready for the night's hunting.

Boobook owls can be found sitting on street lights or on branches in people's gardens.

Boobooks eat mainly insects, such as cockchafer beetles and moths, which swarm around street lights.

Mobbed!

If small birds find a resting owl, they flap and squawk at it to drive it away. After all, when darkness falls it might eat them.

23

Fun facts

Tawny owl The chicks of the tawny owl leave their nest when they are just 4 to 5 weeks old.

Little owl When its chicks first hatch, it is the male little owl's job to feed them.

Snowy owl These fierce owls protect their nests against enemies, even wolves.

Barn owl This owl is found all over the world apart from in the freezing Antarctic.

Scops owl Male scops owls build the nests, and the female chooses her mate depending on which nest she prefers.

Great horned owl When falling asleep, the great horned owl clings to the branch with its talons to stop it falling off.

Eagle owl The male eagle owl's ear tufts point straight up while the female's ear tufts point to the side.

Fishing owl Unlike most owls, the fishing owl has no ear tufts at all.

Elf owl If in danger, the elf owl pretends to be dead and only moves when the danger has passed.

Boobook owl This owl is also known as the spotted hawk owl.

24